Anthony Benezet, James Phillips

A caution to Great Britain and her colonies

Anthony Benezet, James Phillips

A caution to Great Britain and her colonies

ISBN/EAN: 9783337150174

Printed in Europe, USA, Canada, Australia, Japan

Cover: Foto ©ninafisch / pixelio.de

More available books at **www.hansebooks.com**

A

CAUTION

TO

GREAT BRITAIN

AND

HER COLONIES,

IN A

SHORT REPRESENTATION

OF THE

CALAMITOUS STATE of the

ENSLAVED NEGROES

IN THE

BRITISH DOMINIONS.

A NEW EDITION.

By ANTHONY BENEZET.

PHILADELPHIA Printed: LONDON Reprinted and Sold by JAMES PHILLIPS, in George-Yard, Lombard-Street. 1785.

A

CAUTION, &c.

AT a time when the general rights and liberties of mankind, and the prefer-vation of thofe valuable privileges tranfmit-ted to us from our anceftors, are become fo much the fubjects of univerfal confidera-tion; can it be an inquiry indifferent to any, how many of thofe who diftinguifh them-felves as the Advocates of Liberty, remain infenfible and inattentive to the treatment of thoufands and tens of thoufands of our fellow-men, who, from motives of avarice, and the inexorable decree of tyrant cuftom, are at this very time kept in the moft deplorable ftate of Slavery, in many parts of the *Britifh* Dominions?

The intent of publifhing the following fheets, is more fully to make known the aggravated iniquity attending the practice of the Slave-trade; whereby many thoufands of our fellow-creatures, as free as ourfelves by nature, and equally with us the fubjects of

Chrift's

Chrift's redeeming Grace, are yearly brought into inextricable and barbarous bondage; and many, very many, to miferable and untimely ends.

The Truth of this lamentable Complaint is fo obvious to perfons of candour, under whofe notice it hath fallen, that feveral have lately publifhed their fentiments thereon, as a matter which calls for the moft ferious confideration of all who are concerned for the civil or religious welfare of their Country. How an evil of fo deep a dye, hath fo long, not only paffed uninterrupted by thofe in Power, but hath even had their Countenance, is indeed furprifing; and charity would fuppofe, muft in a great meafure have arifen from this, that many perfons in government, both of the Clergy and Laity, in whofe power it hath been to put a ftop to the Trade, have been unacquainted with the corrupt motives which give life to it, and with the groans, the dying groans, which daily afcend to God, the common Father of mankind, from the broken hearts of thofe his deeply oppreffed creatures: otherwife the powers of the earth would not, I think I may venture to fay could not, have fo long authorized a practice fo inconfiftent with every idea of liberty and juftice, which, as the learned *James Fofter* fays, *Bids that God, which is the God and Father of the* Gentiles, *unconverted to* Chriftianity, *moft daring and*

and bold defiance; and spurns at all the prin-
ciples both of natural and revealed Religion.

Much might juftly be faid of the temporal
evils which attend this practice, as it is de-
ftructive of the welfare of human fociety, and
of the peace and profperity of every country,
in proportion at it prevails. It might be alfo
fhewn, that it deftroys the bonds of natural
affection and intereft, whereby mankind in
general are united; that it introduces idlenefs,
difcourages marriage, corrupts the youth, ruins
and debauches morals, excites continual ap-
prehenfions of dangers, and frequent alarms,
to which the Whites are neceffarily expofed
from fo great an increafe of a People, that,
by their Bondage and Oppreffions, become
natural enemies, yet, at the fame time, are
filling the places and eating the bread of thofe
who would be the Support and Security of
the Country. But as thefe and many more
reflections of the fame kind may occur to a
confiderate mind, I fhall only endeavour to
fhew, from the nature of the Trade, the plenty
which *Guinea* affords to its inhabitants, the
barbarous Treatment of the Negroes, and the
Obfervations made thereon by Authors of note,
that it is inconfiftent with the plaineft Precepts
of the Gofpel, the dictates of reafon, and every
common fentiment of humanity.

A 3   In

In an Account of the *European* Settlements in *America*, printed in *London*, 1757, the Author, fpeaking on this Subject, fays: ' The ' Negroes in our Colonies endure a Slavery ' more complete, and attended with far worfe ' circumftances than what any people in their ' condition fuffer in any other part of the ' world, or have fuffered in any other period ' of time: Proofs of this are not wanting. ' The prodigious wafte which we experience ' in this unhappy part of our Species, is a ' full and melancholy Evidence of this Truth. ' The Ifland of *Barbadoes* (the Negroes upon ' which do not amount to eighty thoufand) ' notwithftanding all the means which they ' ufe to encreafe them by Propagation, and ' that the Climate is in every refpect (except ' that of being more wholfome) exactly re- ' fembling the Climate from whence they ' come; notwithftanding all this, *Barbadoes* ' lies under a neceffity of an annual recruit of ' five thoufand flaves, to keep up the ftock at ' the number I have mentioned. This pro- ' digious failure, which is at leaft in the fame ' proportion in all our Iflands, fhews demon- ' ftratively that fome uncommon and unfup- ' portable Hardfhip lies upon the Negroes, ' which wears them down in fuch a furprifing ' manner; and this, I imagine, is principally ' the exceffive labour which they undergo.' In an Account of part of *North-America*, publifhed by *Thomas Jeffery*, 1761, fpeaking
of

of the usage the Negroes receive in the *West-India* Islands, he thus expresses himself: ' It
' is impossible for a human heart to reflect
' upon the servitude of these dregs of man-
' kind, without in some measure feeling for
' their misery, which ends but with their
' lives.——Nothing can be more wretched
' than the condition of this People. One
' would imagine, they were framed to be
' the disgrace of the human species: banished
' from their Country, and deprived of that
' blessing, Liberty, on which all other nations
' set the greatest value, they are in a manner
' reduced to the condition of beasts of bur-
' den. In general a few roots, potatoes es-
' pecially, are their food; and two rags,
' which neither skreen them from the heat
' of the day, nor the extraordinary coolness
' of the night, all their covering; their sleep
' very short; their labour almost continual;
' they receive no wages; but have twenty
' lashes for the smallest fault.'

A considerate young person, who was lately
in one of our *West-India* Islands, where he
observed the miserable situation of the Negroes, makes the following remarks: ' I meet
' with daily exercise, to see the treatment
' which these miserable wretches meet with
' from their masters, with but few exceptions.
' They whip them most unmercifully, on
' small occasions; they beat them with thick

A 4   ' Clubs,

' Clubs, and you will fee their Bodies all
' whaled and fcarred: in fhort, they feem to
' fet no other value on their lives than as they
' coft them fo much money; and are not
' reftrained from killing them, when angry,
' by a worthier confideration than that they
' lofe fo much. They act as though they did
' not look upon them as a race of human
' creatures, who have reafon, and remem-
' brance of misfortunes; but as beafts, like
' oxen, who are ftubborn, hardy, and fenfe-
' lefs, fit for burdens, and defigned to bear
' them. They will not allow them to have
' any claim to human privileges, or fcarce,
' indeed, to be regarded as the work of God.
' Though it was confiftent with the juftice of
' our Maker to pronounce the fentence on
' our common parent, and through him on
' all fucceeding generations, *That he and they*
' *fhould eat their bread by the fweat of their*
' *brow;* yet does it not ftand recorded by the
' fame Eternal Truth, *That the Labourer is*
' *worthy of his Hire?* It cannot be allowed in
' natural juftice, that there fhould be a fervi-
' tude without condition: A cruel endlefs
' fervitude. It cannot be reconcileable to
' natural juftice, that whole nations, nay,
' whole continents of men, fhould be de-
' voted to do the drudgery of life for others,
' be dragged away from their attachments of
' relations and focieties, and made to ferve
' the appetites and pleafures of a race of men,
' whofe

' whofe fuperiority has been obtained by an
' illegal force.'

A particular account of the treatment thefe
unhappy *Africans* receive in the *Weſt-Indies*
was lately publiſhed; which, even by thofe
who, blinded by intereft, feek excufes for the
Trade, and endeavour to palliate the cruelty
exercifed upon them, is allowed to be a true,
though rather too favourable reprefentation of
the ufage they receive, which is as follows,
viz. ' The iniquity of the Slave-trade is
' greatly aggravated by the inhumanity with
' which the Negroes are treated in the Plan-
' tations, as well with refpect to food and
' clothing, as from the unreafonable labour
' which is commonly exacted from them.
' To which may be added the cruel chaftife-
' ments they frequently fuffer, without any
' other bounds than the will and wrath of
' their hard taſk-maſters. In *Barbadoes,* and
' fome other of the Iſlands, fix pints of *Indian*
' corn and three herrings are reckoned a full
' weeks allowance for a working ſlave, and in
' the Syſtem of Geography it is faid, *That in*
' Jamaica *the owners of the Negroe-ſlaves ſet*
' *afide for each a parcel of ground, and allow*
' *them* Sundays *to manure it, the produce of*
' *which,* with fometimes a few herrings, or
' other falt-fiſh, *is all that is allowed for their*
' *fupport.* Their allowance for clothing in
' the Iſlands is feldom more than fix yards of
                              ' ofenbrigs

' ofenbrigs each year: And in th
' ern Colonies, where the pie
' winds are long and fenfibly f(
' *Africans* fuffer much for war
' clothing, indeed fome have
' are able to pay for it by their
' time that the Negroes work
' *Indies*, is from day-break ti
' again from two o'clock till
' which time they are attende(
' who feverely fcourge thofe v
' them dilatory) and before th
' to go to their quarters, they h
' thing to do, as collecting of l
' horfes, gathering fuel for th
' fo that it is often half paft
' they can get home, when th
' time to grind and boil thei
' whereby it often happens
' called again to labour before t
' their hunger. And here no (
' will avail, for if they are nc
' immediately upon the ufual
' muft expect to feel the Overf
' crop-time (which lafts many
' are obliged (by turns) to wo
' night in the boiling-houfe.
' Owners, from a defire of mal
' eft gain by the labour of th
' heavy Burdens on them, anc
' clothe them very fparingly, a
' feed or clothe them at all, fc

' creatures are obliged to fhift for their living,
' in the beft manner they can, which occafions
' their being often killed in the neighbouring
' lands, ftealing potatoes, or other food, to
' fatisfy their hunger. And if they take any
' thing from the plantation they belong to,
' though under fuch prefling want, their
' owners will correct them feverely, for taking
' a little of what they have fo hardly laboured
' for, whilft they themfelves riot in the great-
' eft luxury and excefs.—It is a matter of
' aftonifhment, how a people, who, as a na-
' tion, are looked upon as generous and hu-
' mane, and fo much value themfelves for their
' uncommon fenfe of the Benefit of Liberty,
' can live in the practice of fuch extreme op-
' preffion and inhumanity, without feeing the
' inconfiftency of fuch conduct, and without
' feeling great Remorfe: nor is it lefs amazing
' to hear thefe men calmly making calcula-
' tions about the ftrength and lives of their
' fellow-men; in *Jamaica*, if fix in ten, of the
' new imported Negroes furvive the feafoning,
' it is looked upon as a gaining purchafe: And
' in moft of the other plantations, if the
' Negroes live eight or nine years, their labour
' is reckoned a fufficient compenfation for
' their coft.——If calculations of this fort
' were made upon the ftrength and labour of
' beafts of burden, it would not appear fo
' ftrange; but even then a merciful man would
' certainly ufe his beaft with more mercy than

' is

‘ is usually shewn to the poor Negroes.—Will
‘ not the groans of this deeply afflicted and
‘ oppressed people reach Heaven, and when
‘ the cup of iniquity is full, must not the
‘ inevitable consequence be pouring forth of
‘ the judgments of God upon their oppressors.
‘ But, alas! is it not too manifest that this
‘ oppression has already long been the object
‘ of the divine displeasure; for what heavier
‘ judgment, what greater calamity can befall
‘ any people, than to become a prey to that
‘ hardness of heart, that forgetfulness of God,
‘ and insensibility to every religious impres-
‘ sion; as well as that general depravation of
‘ manners, which so much prevails in the
‘ Colonies, in proportion as they have more or
‘ less enriched themselves, at the expence of
‘ the blood and bondage of the Negroes.’

The situation of the Negroes in our South-
ern provinces on the Continent, is also feel-
ingly set forth by *George Whitfield,* in a
Letter from *Georgia,* to the Inhabitants of
Maryland, Virginia, North and *South-Carolina,*
printed in the Year 1739, of which the following is an extract: ‘ As I lately passed
‘ through your provinces, in my way hither,
‘ I was sensibly touched with a fellow-feeling
‘ of the miseries of the poor Negroes. Whe-
‘ ther it be lawful for *Christians* to buy slaves,
‘ and thereby encourage the Nations from
‘ whom they are bought, to be at perpetual
‘ war

' war with each other, I shall not take upon
' me to determine; sure I am, it is sinful,
' when bought, to use them as bad, nay worse
' than as though they were brutes; and what-
' ever particular exception there may be, (as
' I would charitably hope there are some) I
' fear the generality of you, that own Negroes,
' are liable to such a charge; for your slaves,
' I believe, work as hard, if not harder, than
' the horses whereon you ride. These, after
' they have done their work, are fed and
' taken proper care of; but many Negroes,
' when wearied with labour, in your planta-
' tions, have been obliged to grind their own
' corn, after they return home. Your dogs
' are caressed and fondled at your table; but
' your slaves, who are frequently stiled dogs
' or beasts, have not an equal privilege; they
' are scarce permitted to pick up the crumbs
' which fall from their master's table.—Not
' to mention what numbers have been given
' up to the inhuman usage of cruel task-
' masters, who, by their unrelenting scourges,
' have ploughed their backs, and made long
' furrows, and at length brought them even
' to death. When passing along, I have view-
' ed your plantations cleared and cultivated,
' many spacious houses built, and the owners
' of them faring sumptuously every day, my
' blood has frequently almost run cold within
' me, to consider how many of your slaves had
' neither convenient food to eat, or proper
' raiment

' raiment to put on, notwithftanding moft of
' the comforts you enjoy were folely owing to
' their indefatigable labours.—The Scripture
' fays, *Thou fhalt not muzzle the ox that*
' *treadeth out the corn.* Does God take care
' for oxen? and will he not take care of the
' Negroes alfo? undoubtedly he will.—Go to
' now ye rich men, weep and howl for your
' miferies that fhall come upon you: Behold
' the provifion of the poor Negroes, who have
' reaped down your fields, which is by you
' denied them, crieth; and the cries of them
' which reaped, are entered into the ears of
' the Lord of Sabbath. We have a remark-
' able inftance of God's taking cognizance of,
' and avenging the quarrel of poor flaves,
' 2 Sam. xxi. 1. *There was a famine in the*
' *days of* David *three years, year after year;*
' *and* David *enquired of the Lord: And the*
' *Lord anfwered, It is for* Saul, *and for his*
' *bloody houfe, becaufe he flew the* Gibeonites.
' Two things are here very remarkable: Firft,
' Thefe *Gibeonites* were only hewers of wood
' and drawers of water, or in other words,
' flaves like yours. Secondly, That this plague
' was fent by God many years after the injury,
' the caufe of the plague, was committed.
' And for what end were this and fuch like
' examples recorded in holy Scriptures? with-
' out doubt, for our learning.—For God is
' the fame to-day as he was yefterday, and
' will continue the fame for ever. He does
' not

' not reject the prayer of the poor and defti-
' tute; nor difregard the cry of the meaneft
' Negro. The blood of them fpilt for thefe
' many years in your refpective provinces will
' afcend up to heaven againft you.'

Some who have only feen Negroes in an
abject ftate of flavery, broken-fpirited and
dejected, knowing nothing of their fituation
in their native country, may apprehend, that
they are naturally infenfible of the benefits of
Liberty, being deftitute and miferable in every
refpect, and that our fuffering them to live
amongft us (as the *Gibeonites* of old were
permitted to live with the *Ifraelites*) though
even on more oppreffive terms, is to them a
favour; but thefe are certainly erroneous opi-
nions, with refpect to far the greateft part of
them: Although it is highly probable that in
a country which is more than three thoufand
miles in extent from north to fouth, and as
much from eaft to weft, there will be barren
parts, and many inhabitants more uncivilized
and barbarous than others; as is the cafe in all
other countries: yet, from the moft authen-
tic accounts, the inhabitants of *Guinea* appear,
generally fpeaking, to be an induftrious, humane, fociable people, whofe capacities are
naturally as enlarged, and as open to improve-
ment, as thofe of the *Europeans*; and that
their Country is fruitful, and in many places
well improved, abounding in cattle, grain and
fruits.

fruits. And as the earth yields all the year
round a fresh supply of food, and but little
clothing is requisite, by reason of the continual warmth of the climate; the neceffaries
of life are much easier procured in most parts
of *Africa*, than in our more northern climes.
This is confirmed by many authors of note,
who have resided there; among others, *M.
Adanson*, in his account of *Goree* and *Senegal*,
in the year 1754, says, ' Which way foever
' I turned my eyes on this pleasant spot, I
' beheld a perfect image of pure nature; an
' agreeable solitude, bounded on every side by
' charming landscapes, the rural situation of
' cottages in the midst of trees; the ease and
' indolence of the Negroes reclined under the
' shade of their spreading foliage; the simpli-
' city of their dress and manners; the whole
' revived in my mind the idea of our first
' parents, and I seemed to contemplate the
' world in its primitive state: They are, gene-
' rally speaking, very good-natured, sociable
' and obliging. I was not a little pleased with
' this my first reception; it convinced me,
' that there ought to be a considerable abate-
' ment made in the accounts I had read and
' heard every where of the savage character of
' the *Africans*. I observed, both in Negroes
' and Moors, great humanity and sociableness,
' which gave me strong hopes, that I should
' be very safe amongst them, and meet with
                                        ' the

' the fuccefs I defired, in my enquiries after
' the curiofities of the country.'

William Bofman, a principal Factor for the
Dutch, who refided fixteen years in *Guinea*,
fpeaking of the natives of that part where he
then was, fays, ' They are generally a good
' fort of people, honeft in their dealings;'
others he defcribes as ' being generally friendly
' to ftrangers, of a mild converfation, affable,
' and eafy to be overcome with reafon.' He
adds, ' That fome Negroes, who have had
' an agreeable education, have manifefted a
' brightnefs of underftanding equal to any of
' us.' Speaking of the fruitfulnefs of the
country, he fays, ' It was very populous,
' plentifully provided with corn, potatoes and
' fruit, which grew clofe to each other; in
' fome places a foot-path is the only ground
' that is not covered with them; the Negroes
' leaving no place, which is thought fertile,
' uncultivated; and immediately after they
' have reaped, they are fure to fow again.'
Other parts he defcribes, as ' being full of
' towns and villages; the foil very rich, and
' fo well cultivated, as to look like an entire
' garden, abounding in rice, corn, oxen, and
' poultry, and the inhabitants laborious.'

William Smith, who was fent by the *African* Company to vifit their fettlements on the
coaft of *Guinea*, in the year 1726, gives much
B   the

the fame account of the country of *Delmina* and *Cape Corfe*, &c. for beauty and goodnefs, and adds, ' The more you come downward ' towards that part, called *Slave-Coaft*, the ' more delightful and rich the foil appears.' Speaking of their difpofition, he fays, ' They ' were a civil, good-natured people, induf- ' trious to the laft degree. It is eafy to perceive ' what happy memories they are bleffed with, ' and how great progrefs they would make in ' the fciences, in cafe their genius was cul- ' tivated with ftudy.' He adds, from the in- formation he received of one of the Factors, who had refided ten years in that country, ' That the difcerning natives account it their ' greateft unhappinefs, that they were ever ' vifited by the *Europeans.*—That the *Chrif-* ' *tians* introduced the traffick of Slaves; and ' that before our coming they lived in peace.'

Andrew Brue, a principal man in the *French* Factory, in the account he gives of the great river *Senegal*, which runs many hundred miles up the country, tells his readers, ' The farther ' you go from the Sea, the country on the ' river feems more fruitful and well improved. ' It abounds in *Guinea* and *Indian* corn, rice, ' pulfe, tobacco, and indigo. Here are vaft ' meadows, which feed large herds of great ' and fmall cattle; poultry are numerous, as ' well as wild fowl.' The fame Author, in his travels to the fouth of the river *Gambia*, exprefies

expreffes his furprize, 'to fee the land fo well
' cultivated; fcarce a fpot lay unimproved;
' the low grounds, divided by fmall canals,
' were all fowed with rice; the higher ground
' planted with *Indian* corn, millet, and peas
' of different forts: beef and mutton very
' cheap, as well as all other neceffaries of life.'
The account this Author gives of the difpofition of the natives, is, ' That they are gene-
' rally good-natured and civil, and may be
' brought to any thing by fair and foft means.'
Artus, fpeaking of the fame people, fays,
' They are a fincere, inoffenfive people, and
' do no injuftice either to one another, or
' ftrangers.'

From thefe Accounts, both of the good
Difpofition of the Natives, and the Fruitfulnefs of moft parts of *Guinea*, which are confirmed by many other Authors, it may well
be concluded, that their acquaintance with
the *Europeans* would have been a happinefs
to them, had thofe laft not only borne the
name, but indeed been influenced by the
Spirit of *Chriftianity*; but, alas! how hath
the Conduct of the Whites contradicted the
Precepts and Example of Chrift? Inftead of
promoting the End of his Coming, by preach-
ing the Gofpel of Peace and Good-will to
Man, they have, by their practices, contri-
buted to enflame every noxious paffion of
corrupt nature in the Negroes; they have

B 2   incited

incited them to make war one upon another, and for this purpose have furnished them with prodigious quantities of ammunition and arms, whereby they have been hurried into confusion, bloodshed, and all the extremities of temporal misery, which must necessarily beget in their minds such a general detestation and scorn of the *Christian* name, as may deeply affect, if not wholly preclude, their belief of the great Truths of our holy Religion. Thus an insatiable desire of gain hath become the principal and moving cause of the most abominable and dreadful scene, that was perhaps ever acted upon the face of the earth; even the power of their Kings hath been made subservient to answer this wicked purpose; instead of being Protectors of their people, these Rulers, allured by the tempting bait laid before them by the *European* Factors, &c. have invaded the Liberties of their unhappy subjects, and are become their Oppressors.

Divers accounts have already appeared in print, declarative of the shocking wickedness with which this Trade is carried on; these may not have fallen into the hands of some of my readers, I shall, therefore, for their information, select a few of the most remarkable instances that I have met with, shewing the method by which the Trade is commonly managed all along the *African* coast.

Francis

Francis Moor, Factor to the *African* Company, on the river *Gambia,* relates, ' That
' when the King of *Barfalli* wants goods, *&c.*
' he fends a meffenger to the *English* Governor
' at *James*'s Fort, to defire he would fend up
' a floop with a cargo of goods; which (fays
' the author) the Governor never fails to do:
' Againft the time the veffel arrives, the King
' plunders fome of his enemies towns, felling
' the people for fuch goods as he wants.——
' If he is not at war with any neighbouring
' King, he falls upon one of his own towns,
' and makes bold to fell his own miferable
' fubjects.'

N. Brue, in his account of the Trade, *&c.*
writes, ' That having received a quantity of
' goods, he wrote to the King of the country,
' That if he had a fufficient number of flaves,
' he was ready to trade with him. This
' Prince (fays that author) as well as other
' Negroe Monarchs, has always a fure way
' of fupplying his deficiencies by felling his
' own fubjects.——The King had recourfe to
' this method, by feizing three hundred of
' his own people, and fent word (to *Brue,*)
' that he had the flaves ready to deliver for
' the goods.'

The Mifery and Bloodfhed, confequent to
the Slave-trade, is amply fet forth by the following extracts of two voyages to the coaft
of

of *Guinea* for flaves. The firft in a veffel from
Liverpool, taken *verbatim* from the original
manufcript of the Surgeon's journal, *viz.*

' SESTRO, *December* the 29th, 1724. No
' trade to-day, though many Traders come
' on board; they inform us, that the people
' are gone to war within land, and will bring
' prifoners enough in two or three days: in
' hopes of which we ftay.

' The 30th. No trade yet, but our Traders
' came on board to-day, and informed us,
' the people had burnt four towns of their
' enemies, fo that to-morrow we expect flaves
' off. Another large fhip is come in: Yefter-
' day came in a large *Londoner*.

' The 31ft. Fair weather, but no trade
' yet: We fee each night towns burning;
' but we hear the *Seftro* men are many of
' them killed by the inland Negroes, fo that
' we fear this war will be unfuccefsful.

' The 2d *January*. Laft night we faw a
' prodigious fire break out about eleven
' o'clock, and this morning fee the town of
' *Seftro* burnt down to the ground, (it con-
' tained fome hundreds of houfes) fo that we
' find their enemies are too hard for them at
' prefent, and confequently our trade fpoiled
' here; fo that about feven o'clock we
                                    ' weighed

'weighed anchor, as did likewife the three
'other veffels, to proceed lower down.'

The fecond relation, alfo taken from the
original manufcript journal of a perfon of
credit, who went Surgeon on the fame account in a veffel from *New-York* to the coaft
of *Guinea*, about nineteen years paft, is as
follows, *viz.*

'Being on the coaft at a place called
'*Bafalia*, the Commander of the veffel, ac-
'cording to cuftom, fent a perfon on fhore
'with a prefent to the King, acquainting
'him with his arrival, and letting him know,
'they wanted a cargo of flaves. The King
'promifed to furnifh them with flaves; and
'in order to do it, fet out to go to war againft
'his enemies, defigning alfo to furprize fome
'town, and take all the people prifoners:
'Some time after, the King fent them word,
'he had not yet met with the defired fuccefs,
'having been twice repulfed, in attempting
'to break up two towns; but that he ftill
'hoped to procure a number of flaves for
'them; and in this defign he perfifted till
'he met his enemies in the field, where a
'battle was fought, which lafted three days;
'during which time the engagement was fo
'bloody, that four thoufand five hundred
'men were flain on the fpot.' The perfon,
that wrote the account, beheld the bodies as

they

they lay on the field of battle. ' Think (fays
' he in his journal) what a pitiable fight it
' was, to fee the widows weeping over their
' loft hufbands, orphans deploring the lofs
' of their fathers, &c. &c.'

Thofe who are acquainted with the Trade
agree, that many Negroes on the fea-coaft,
who have been corrupted by their intercourfe
and converfe with the *European* Factors, have
learnt to ftick at no act of cruelty for gain.
Thefe make it a practice to fteal abundance
of little Blacks of both fexes, when found on
the roads or in the fields, where their parents
keep them all day to watch the corn, &c.
Some authors fay, the Negroe Factors go fix
or feven hundred miles up the country with
goods, bought from the *Europeans,* where
markets of men are kept in the fame manner
as thofe of beafts with us. When the poor
flaves, whether brought from far or near,
come to the fea-fhore, they are ftripped
naked, and ftrictly examined by the *European*
Surgeons, both men and women, without
the leaft diftinction or modefty; thofe which
are approved as good, are marked with a red-
hot iron with the fhip's mark; after which
they are put on board the veffels, the men
being fhackled with irons two and two together. Reader, bring the matter home,
and confider whether any fituation in life can
be more completely miferable than that of
thofe

thofe diftreffed captives. When we reflect, that each individual of this number had fome tender attachment which was broken by this cruel feparation; fome parent or wife, who had not an opportunity of mingling tears in a parting embrace; perhaps fome infant or aged parent whom his labour was to feed and vigilance protect; themfelves under the dreadful apprehenfion of an unknown perpetual flavery; pent up within the narrow confines of a veffel, fometimes fix or feven hundred together, where they lie as clofe as poffible. Under thefe complicated diftreffes they are often reduced to a ftate of defperation, wherein many have leaped into the fea, and have kept themfelves under water till they were drowned; others have ftarved themfelves to death, for the prevention whereof fome mafters of veffels have cut off the legs and arms of a number of thofe poor defperate creatures, to terrify the reft. Great numbers have alfo frequently been killed, and fome deliberately put to death under the greateft torture, when they have attempted to rife, in order to free themfelves from their prefent mifery, and the flavery defigned them. An inftance of the laft kind appears particularly in an account given by the mafter of a veffel, who brought a cargo of flaves to *Barbadoes*; indeed it appears fo irreconcileable to the common dictates of humanity, that one would doubt the truth

of

of it, had it not been related by a ferious
perfon of undoubted credit, who had it from
the captain's own mouth. Upon an enquiry,
What had been the fuccefs of his voyage?
he anfwered, ' That he had found it a diffi-
' cult matter to fet the negroes a fighting
' with each other, in order to procure the
' number he wanted; but that when he had
' obtained this end, and had got his veffel
' filled with flaves, a new difficulty arofe
' from their refufal to take food; thofe def-
' perate creatures chufing rather to die with
' hunger, than to be carried from their native
' country.' Upon a farther inquiry, by what
means he had prevailed upon them to fore-
go this defperate refolution? he anfwered,
' That he obliged all the negroes to come
' upon deck, where they perfifted in their
' refolution of not taking food, he caufed his
' failors to lay hold upon one of the moft
' obftinate, and chopt the poor creature into
' fmall pieces, forcing fome of the others to
' eat a part of the mangled body; withal
' fwearing to the furvivors that he would
' ufe them all, one after the other, in the
' fame manner, if they did not confent to
' eat.' This horrid execution he applauded
as a good act, it having had the defired effect,
in bringing them to take food.

A fimilar cafe is mentioned in *Aftley*'s
Collection of Voyages, by *John Atkins*, Surgeon

geon on board Admiral *Ogle*'s fquadron, ' Of
' one *Harding*, mafter of a veffel, in which
' feveral of the men-flaves, and a woman-
' flave, had attempted to rife, in order to
' recover their liberty: fome of whom the
' mafter, of his own authority, fentenced to
' cruel death; making them firft eat the
' heart and liver of one of thofe he killed.
' The woman he hoifted by the thumbs;
' whipped and flafhed with knives before the
' other flaves, till fhe died.'

As deteftable and fhocking as this may appear to fuch, whofe hearts are not yet hard-
ened by the practice of that cruelty, which
the love of wealth, by degrees, introduceth
into the human mind; it will not be ftrange
to thofe who have been concerned or employed in the Trade. Now here arifes a neceffary
query to thofe who hold the balance and
fword of juftice; and who muft account to
God for the ufe they have made of it. *Since
our English law is fo truly valuable for its
juftice, how can they overlook thefe barbarous
deaths of the unhappy Africans without trial,
or due proof of their being guilty, of crimes
adequate to their punifhment? Why are thofe
mafters of veffels, (who are often not the moft
tender and confiderate of men) thus fuffered
to be the fovereign arbiters of the lives of the
miferable Negroes; and allowed, with impu-
nity, thus to deftroy, may I not fay, murder*
their

their fellow-creatures, and that by means so cruel, as cannot be even related but with shame and horror?

When the vessels arrive at their destined port in the Colonies, the poor Negroes are to be disposed of to the planters; and here they are again exposed naked, without any distinction of sexes, to the brutal examination of their purchasers; and this, it may well be judged, is to many of them another occasion of deep distress, especially to the females. Add to this, that near connections must now again be separated, to go with their several purchasers: In this melancholy scene Mothers are seen hanging over their Daughters, bedewing their naked breasts with tears, and Daughters clinging to their Parents; not knowing what new stage of distress must follow their separation, or if ever they shall meet again: And here what sympathy, what commiseration are they to expect? why indeed, if they will not separate as readily as their owners think proper, the whipper is called for, and the lash exercised upon their naked bodies, till obliged to part.

Can any human heart, that retains a fellow-feeling for the Sufferings of mankind, be unconcerned at relations of such grievous affliction, to which this oppressed part of our Species are subjected: God gave to man
dominion

dominion over the fish of the sea, and over the fowls of the air, and over the cattle, &c. but imposed no involuntary subjection of one man to another.

The Truth of this Position has of late been clearly set forth by persons of reputation and ability, particularly *George Wallis,* in his System of the Laws of *Scotland,* whose sentiments are so worthy the notice of all considerate persons, that I shall here repeat a part of what he has not long since published, concerning the *African* Trade, *viz.* ' If this ' Trade admits of a moral or a rational justi- ' fication, every crime, even the most atro- ' cious, may be justified: Government was ' instituted for the good of mankind. Kings, ' Princes, Governors, are not proprietors of ' those who are subjected to their authority, ' they have not a right to make them miser- ' able. On the contrary, their authority is ' vested in them, that they may, by the just ' exercise of it, promote the Happiness of ' their people: Of course, they have not a ' right to dispose of their Liberty, and to sell ' them for slaves: Besides, no man has a ' right to acquire or to purchase them; men ' and their Liberty, are not either saleable or ' purchaseable: One therefore has no body ' but himself to blame, in case he shall ' find himself deprived of a man, whom he ' thought he had, by buying for a price,
' made

' made his own; for he dealt in a Trade
' which was illicit, and was prohibited by
' the moſt obvious dictates of humanity. For
' theſe reaſons, every one of thoſe unfortunate
' men, who are pretended to be ſlaves, has
' a right to be declared free, for he never
' loſt his Liberty, he could not loſe it; his
' Prince had no power to diſpoſe of him:
' of courſe the ſale was void. This right
' he carries about with him, and is entitled
' every where to get it declared. As ſoon,
' therefore, as he comes into a country, in
' which the Judges are not forgetful of their
' own humanity, it is their duty to remember
' that he is a man, and to declare him to be
' free.—This is the Law of Nature, which
' is obligatory on all men, at all times, and
' in all places.—Would not any of us, who
' ſhould be ſnatched by Pirates from his
' native land, think himſelf cruelly abuſed,
' and at all times intitled to be free? Have
' not theſe unfortunate *Africans*, who meet
' with the ſame cruel fate, the ſame right?
' are not they men as well as we? and have
' they not the ſame ſenſibility? Let us not,
' therefore, defend or ſupport an uſage, which
' is contrary to all the Laws of Humanity.'

Francis Hutchinſon, alſo in his Syſtem of
Moral Philoſophy, ſpeaking on the ſubject of
Slavery, ſays, ' He who detains another by
' force in ſlavery, is always bound to prove
' his

‘ his title, The Slave fold, or carried away
‘ into a diftant country, muft not be obliged
‘ to prove a negative, that he never forfeited
‘ his Liberty. The violent poffeffor muft, in
‘ all cafes, fhew his title, efpecially where the
‘ old proprietor is well known. In this cafe
‘ each man is the original proprietor of his
‘ own Liberty: The proof of his lofing it
‘ muft be incumbent on thofe, who deprived
‘ him of it by force. Strange, (fays the fame
‘ author) that in any nation, where a fenfe of
‘ Liberty prevails, where the *Chriftian* religion
‘ is profeffed, cuftom and high profpect of
‘ gain can fo ftupify the confciences of men,
‘ and all fenfe of natural juftice, that they can
‘ hear fuch computation made about the value
‘ of their fellow-men and their Liberty,
‘ without abhorrence and indignation.’

The noted Baron *Montefquieu* gives it, as
his opinion, in his *Spirit of Laws,* page 348,
‘ That nothing more affimilates a man to a
‘ beaft than living amongft freemen, himfelf
‘ a flave; fuch people as thefe are the natural
‘ enemies of fociety, and their number muft
‘ always be dangerous.’

The Author of a pamphlet, lately printed
in *London,* entitled, *An Effay in Vindication
of the continental Colonies of* America, writes,
‘ That the bondage we have impofed on the
‘ *Africans,* is abfolutely repugnant to juftice:
‘ That

' That it is highly inconsistent with civil
' policy: First, as it tends to suppress all
' improvements in arts and sciences; without
' which it is morally impossible that any
' nation should be happy or powerful. Se-
' condly, as it may deprave the minds of the
' freemen; steeling their hearts against the
' laudable feelings of virtue and humanity.
' And, lastly, as it endangers the community
' by the destructive effects of civil commo-
' tions: need I add to these (says that author)
' what every heart, which is not callous to
' all tender feelings, will readily suggest; that
' it is shocking to humanity, violative of every
' generous sentiment, abhorrent utterly from
' the *Christian* Religion: for, as *Montesquieu*
' very justly observes, *We must suppose them*
' *not to be men, or a suspicion would follow*
' *that we ourselves are not* Christians.———
' There cannot be a more dangerous maxim,
' than that necessity is a plea for injustice.
' For who shall fix the degree of this neces-
' sity? What villain so atrocious, who may
' not urge this excuse? or, as *Milton* has
' happily expressed it,

' ——————————— *And with necessity,*
' *The tyrant's plea, excuse his dev'lish deed.*

' That our Colonies want people, is a very
' weak argument for so inhuman a violation
' of justice.——Shall a civilized, a *Christian*
' nation encourage Slavery, because the bar-
' barous

' barous, favage, lawlefs *African* hath done
' it? Monftrous thought! To what end do
' we profefs a religion whofe dictates we fo
' flagrantly violate? Wherefore have we that
' pattern of goodnefs and humanity, if we
' refufe to follow it? How long fhall we
' continue a practice, which policy rejects,
' juftice condemns, and piety diffuades? Shall
' the *Americans* perfift in a conduct, which
' cannot be juftified; or perfevere in oppref-
' fion from which their hearts muft recoil?
' If the barbarous *Africans* fhall continue to
' enflave each other, let the dæmon flavery
' remain among them, that their crime may
' include its own punifhment. Let not
' *Chriftians*, by adminiftering to their wick-
' ednefs, confefs their religion to be a ufelefs
' refinement, their profeffion vain, and them-
' felves as inhuman as the favages they deteft.'

James Fofter, in *his Difcourfes on Natural
Religion and Social Virtue*, alfo fhews his juft
indignation at this wicked practice, which he
declares to be *a criminal and outrageous violation of the natural right of mankind.* At
page 156, 2d vol. he fays, ' Should we have
' read concerning the *Greeks* or *Romans* of
' old, that they traded, with view to make
' flaves of their own fpecies, whom they
' certainly knew that this would involve in
' fchemes of blood and murder, of deftroy-
' ing or enflaving each other, that they even

C   ' foment-

' fomented wars, and engaged whole nations
' and tribes in open hoftilities, for their own
' private advantage; that they had no detefta-
' tion of the violence and cruelty, but only
' feared the ill fuccefs of their inhuman en-
' terprifes; that they carried men like them-
' felves, their brethren, and the offspring of
' the fame common parent, to be fold like
' beafts of prey, or beafts of burden, and
' put them to the fame reproachful trial of
' their foundnefs, ftrength and capacity for
' greater bodily fervice; that quite forgetting
' and renouncing the original dignity of
' human nature, communicated to all, they
' treated them with more feverity and ruder
' difcipline, than even the ox or the afs, who
' are void of underftanding.—Should we not,
' if this had been the cafe, have naturally
' been led to defpife all their pretended refine-
' ments of morality; and to have concluded,
' that as they were not nations deftitute of
' politenefs, they muft have been *entire*
' *Strangers to Virtue and Benevolence?*

' But, notwithftanding this, we ourfelves
' (who profefs to be *Chriftians,* and boaft of
' the peculiar advantage we enjoy, by means
' of an exprefs revelation of our duty from
' Heaven) are in effect, thefe very untaught
' and rude *Heathen* countries. With all our
' fuperior light, we inftil into thofe, whom
' we call favage and barbarous, the moft
' defpicable

' defpicable opinion of human nature. We,
' to the utmoft of our power, weaken and
' diffolve the univerfal tie, that binds and
' unites mankind. We practife what we
' fhould exclaim againft, as the utmoft excefs
' of cruelty and tyranny, if nations of the
' world, differing in colour and form of
' government from ourfelves, were fo poffef-
' fed of empire, as to be able to reduce us to
' a ftate of unmerited and brutifh fervitude.
' Of confequence, we facrifice our reafon, our
' humanity, our *Chriftianity*, to an unnatural
' fordid gain. We teach other nations to
' defpife and trample under foot, all the obli-
' gations of focial virtue. We take the moft
' effectual method to prevent the propagation
' of the Gofpel, by reprefenting it as a fcheme
' of power and barbarous oppreffion, and an
' enemy to the natural privileges and rights
' of men.

' Perhaps all that I have now offered, may
' be of very little weight to reftrain this enor-
' mity, this aggravated iniquity. However,
' I fhall ftill have the fatisfaction, of having
' entered my private proteft againft a practice,
' which, in my opinion, *bids that God, who*
' *is the God and Father of the* Gentiles *un-*
' *converted to* Chriftianity, *moft daring and*
' *bold defiance, and fpurns at all the principles,*
' *both of natural and revealed Religion.*'

How the *Britiſh* nation firſt came to be concerned in a practice, by which the rights and liberties of mankind are ſo violently infringed, and which is ſo oppoſite to the apprehenſions *Engliſhmen* have always had of what natural juſtice requires, is indeed ſurpriſing. It was about the year 1563, in the reign of Queen *Elizabeth*, that the *Engliſh* firſt engaged in the *Guinea* Trade; when it appears, from an account in *Hill*'s Naval Hiſtory, page 293, That when Captain *Hawkins* returned from his firſt voyage to *Africa*, that generous ſpirited Princeſs, attentive to the intereſt of her ſubjects, ſent for the Commander, to whom ſhe expreſſed her concern left any of the *African* Negroes ſhould be carried off without their free conſent, *declaring it would be deteſtable, and call down the vengeance of Heaven upon the undertakers.* Captain *Hawkins* promiſed to comply with the Queen's injunction: nevertheleſs, we find in the account, given in the ſame Hiſtory, of *Hawkins*'s ſecond voyage, the author uſing theſe remarkable words, *Here began the horrid practice of forcing the* Africans *into ſlavery.*

Labat, a *Roman* Miſſionary, in his account of the Iſles of *America*, at page 114, of the 4th vol. mentions, that *Lewis* the 13th, Father to the preſent *French* King's Grandfather, was extremely uneaſy at a Law by which all the Negroes of his Colonies were

to

to be made flaves; but it being ftrongly
urged to him, as the readieft means for
their Converfion to *Chriftianity*, he acqui-
efced therewith.

And although we have not many accounts
of the impreffions which this piratical invafion of the rights of mankind gave to ferious
minded people, when firft engaged in; yet
it did not efcape the notice of fome, who
might be efteemed in a peculiar manner as
watchmen in their day to the different focieties of *Chriftians* whereunto they belonged.
Richard Baxter, an eminent preacher amongft
the *Nonconformifts*, in the laft century, well
known and particularly efteemed by moft
of the ferious *Prefbyterians* and *Independents*,
in his *Chriftian* Directory, moftly wrote about
an hundred Years ago, fully fhews his detefta-
tion of this practice in the following words:
' Do you not mark how God hath followed
' you with plagues? And may not confcience
' tell you, that it is for your inhumanity to
' the fouls and bodies of men?—To go as
' pirates and catch up poor Negroes, or peo-
' ple of another land, that never forfeited
' Life or Liberty, and to make them Slaves
' and fell them, is one of the worft kind of
' Thievery in the world; and fuch perfons
' are to be taken for the common Enemies
' of mankind; and they that buy them, and
' ufe them as beafts, for their meer com-

C 3   ' modity,

' modity, and betray, or deftroy, or neglect
' their fouls, are fitter to be called devils than
' *Chriftians*. It is an heinous fin to buy them,
' unlefs it be in charity to deliver them.——
' Undoubtedly they are prefently bound to
' deliver them; becaufe by right the man is
' his own; therefore no man elfe can have a
' juft title to him.'

We alfo find *George Fox*, a man of exem-
plary piety, who was the principal inftrument
in gathering the religious fociety of people
called *Quakers*, expreffing his concern and
fellow-feeling for the bondage of the Negroes:
In a difcourfe taken from his mouth, in
Barbadoes, in the Year 1671, fays, ' Confi-
' der with yourfelves, if you were in the
' fame condition as the Blacks are,—who
' came ftrangers to you, and were fold to you
' as flaves. I fay, if this fhould be the con-
' dition of you or yours, you would think it
' hard meafure: Yea, and very great bondage
' and cruelty. And, therefore, confider fe-
' rioufly of this, and do you for and to them,
' as you would willingly have them, or any
' other to do unto you, were you in the like
' flavifh condition; and bring them to know
' the Lord Chrift.' And in his journal, page
431, fpeaking of the Advice he gave his
friends at *Barbadoes*, he fays, ' I defired alfo,
' that they would caufe their Overfeers to deal
' mildly and gently with their Negroes, and
' not

' not to ufe cruelty towards them, as the
' manner of fome had been; and that after
' certain years of fervitude they fhould make
' them free.'

In a book printed in *Leverpool*, called *The Leverpool Memorandum-book*, which contains, among other things, an account of the Trade of that port, there is an exact lift of the veffels employed in the *Guinea* Trade, and of the number of Slaves imported in each veffel, by which it appears, that in the year 1753, the number imported to *America*, by veffels belonging to that port, amounted to upwards of Thirty Thoufand; and from the number of Veffels employed by the *African* Company in *London* and *Briftol*, we may, with fome degree of certainty conclude, there is, at leaft, One Hundred Thoufand Negroes purchafed and brought on board our fhips yearly from the coaft of *Africa*, on their account. This is confirmed in *Anderfon*'s Hiftory of Trade and Commerce, printed in 1764, where it is faid, at page 68 of the Appendix, ' That *England* fupplies her *Ame-*' *rican* Colonies with Negro-flaves, amount-' ing in number to above One Hundred ' Thoufand every year.' When the veffels are full freighted with flaves, they fet out for our plantations in *America*, and may be two or three months on the voyage, during which time, from the filth and ftench that is

among

among them, diftempers frequently break out,
which carry off a great many, a fifth, a fourth,
yea, fometimes a third of them; fo that taking
all the flaves together that are brought on
board our fhips yearly, one may reafonably
fuppofe, that at leaft ten thoufand of them die
on the voyage. And in a printed account of
the State of the Negroes in our plantations, it
is fuppofed that a fourth part, more or lefs,
die at the different Iflands, in what is called
the feafoning. Hence it may be prefumed,
that, at a moderate computation of the flaves,
who are purchafed by our *African* merchants
in a year, near thirty thoufand die upon the
voyage and in the feafoning. Add to this, the
prodigious number who are killed in the
incurfions and inteftine wars, by which the
Negroes procure the number of flaves wanted
to load the veffels. How dreadful then is this
Slave-Trade, whereby fo many thoufands of
our fellow-creatures, free by nature, endued
with the fame rational faculties, and called to
be heirs of the fame falvation with us, lofe
their lives, and are truly, and properly fpeaking, murdered every year! For it is not
neceffary, in order to convict a man of
murder, to make it appear, that he had an
intention to commit murder. Whoever does,
by unjuft force or violence, deprive another
of his Liberty; and, while he has him in his
power, reduces him, by cruel treatment, to
fuch a condition as evidently endangers his
life,

life; and the event occasions his death, is
actually guilty of murder. It is no less shocking to read the accounts given by Sir *Hans
Sloane*, and others, of the inhuman and un-
merciful treatment those Blacks meet with,
who survive the seasonings in the Islands, often
for transgressions, to which the punishment
they receive bears no proportion. ‘ And the
‘ horrid executions, which are frequently
‘ made there upon discovery of the plots laid
‘ by the Blacks, for the recovery of their
‘ liberty; of some they break the bones,
‘ whilst alive, on a wheel; others they burn
‘ or rather roast to death; others they starve
‘ to death, with a loaf hanging before their
‘ mouths.’ Thus they are brought to expire,
with frightful agonies, in the most horrid
tortures. For negligence only they are unmercifully whipped, till their backs are raw,
and then pepper and salt is scattered on the
wounds to heighten the pain, and prevent
mortification. Is it not a cause of much sor-
row and lamentation, that so many poor creatures should be thus racked with excrucia-
ting tortures, for crimes which often their
tormentors have occasioned? Must not even
the common feelings of human nature have
suffered some grievous change in those men,
to be capable of such horrid cruelty towards
their fellow-men? If they deserve death,
ought not their judges, in the death decreed
them,

them, always to remember that thefe their haplefs fellow-creatures are men, and themfelves profeffing *Chriftians?* The *Mofaic* law teaches us our duty in thefe cafes, in the merciful provifion it made in the punifhment of tranfgreffors, *Deuter.* xxv. 2. *And it fhall be, if the wicked man be worthy to be beaten, that the judge fhall caufe him to lie down, and to be beaten before his face, according to his fault, by a certain number; Forty ftripes he may give him, and not exceed.* And the reafon rendered is out of refpect to human nature, *viz. Left if he fhould exceed, and beat him above thefe, with many ftripes, then thy Brother fhould feem vile unto thee.* *Britains* boaft themfelves to be a generous, humane people, who have a true fenfe of the importance of Liberty; but is this a true character, whilft that barbarous, favage Slave-Trade, with all its attendant horrors, receives countenance and protection from the Legiflature, whereby fo many Thoufand lives are yearly facrificed? Do we indeed believe the truths declared in the Gofpel? Are we perfuaded that the threatenings, as well as the promifes therein contained, will have their accomplifhment? If indeed we do, muft we not tremble to think what a load of guilt lies upon our Nation generally, and individually, fo far as we in any degree abet or countenance this aggravated iniquity?

We

We have a memorable Inftance in hiftory, which may be fruitful of Inftruction, if timely and properly applied; it is a quotation made by Sir *John Temple*, in his hiftory of the *Irifh* rebellion, being an obfervation out of *Giraldus Cambrenfis*, a noted author, who lived about fix hundred years ago, concerning the caufes of the profperity of the *Englifh* undertakings in *Ireland*, when they conquered that Ifland, he faith, ' That a fy-
' nod, or council of the Clergy, being then
' affembled at *Armagh*, and that point fully
' debated, it was unanimoufly agreed, that
' the fins of the people were the occafion of
' that heavy judgment then falling upon
' their nation; and that efpecially their
' buying of *Englifhmen* from merchants and
' pirates, and detaining them under a moft
' miferable hard bondage, had caufed the
' Lord, by way of juft retaliation, to leave
' them to be reduced, by the *Englifh*, to the
' fame ftate of flavery. Whereupon they
' made a publick act in that council, that all
' the *Englifh*, held in captivity throughout
' the whole land, fhould be prefently re-
' ftored to their former Liberty.'

I fhall now conclude with an extract from an addrefs of a late author to the merchants, and others, who are concerned in carrying on the *Guinea* Trade; which alfo, in a great meafure,

meafure, is applicable to others, who, for
the love of gain, are in any way concerned
in promoting or maintaining the captivity of
the Negroes.

    ' As the bufinefs, you are publickly carry-
' ing on before the world, has a bad afpect,
' and you are fenfible moft men make objec-
' tion againft it, you ought to juftify it to
' the world, upon principles of reafon,
' equity, and humanity; to make it appear,
' that it is no unjuft invafion of the perfons,
' or encroachments on the rights of men; or
' for ever to lay it afide.—But laying afide
' the refentment of men, which is but of
' little or no moment, in comparifon with
' that of the Almighty, think of a future
' reckoning: confider how you fhall come
' off in the great and awful Day of account.
' You now heap up riches, and live in plea-
' fure; but, oh! what will you do in the end
' thereof? and that is not far off: what, if
' death fhould feize upon you, and hurry you
' out of this world, under all that load of
' blood-guiltinefs that now lies upon your
' fouls ? The gofpel exprefly declares, that
' thieves and murderers fhall not inherit the
' kingdom of God. Confider, that at the
' fame time, and by the fame means, you
' now treafure up worldly riches, you are
' treafuring up to yourfelves wrath againft
                            ' the

‘ the day of wrath, and vengeance that ſhall
‘ come upon the workers of iniquity, unleſs
‘ prevented by a timely repentance.

‘ And what greater iniquity, what crime
‘ that is more heinous, that carries in it more
‘ complicated guilt, can you name than that,
‘ in the habitual, deliberate practice of which
‘ you now live? How can you lift up your
‘ guilty eyes to heaven? How can you pray
‘ for mercy to him that made you, or hope
‘ for any favour from him that formed you,
‘ while you go on thus groſly and openly to
‘ diſhonour him, in debaſing and deſtroying
‘ the nobleſt workmanſhip of his hands in
‘ this lower world? He is the Father of men;
‘ and do you think he will not reſent ſuch
‘ treatment of his offspring, whom he hath
‘ ſo loved, as to give his only begotten Son,
‘ that whoſoever believeth in him, might not
‘ periſh, but have everlaſting life? This love
‘ of God to man, revealed in the goſpel, is a
‘ great aggravation of your guilt; for if God
‘ ſo loved us, we ought alſo to love one ano-
‘ ther. *You remember the fate of the Servant,*
‘ *who took hold of his fellow-ſervant, who*
‘ *was in his debt, by the throat, and caſt him*
‘ *into priſon:* Think then, and tremble to
‘ think, what will be your fate, who take
‘ your fellow-ſervants by the throat, that
‘ owe you not a penny, and make them
‘ priſoners for life.

‘ Give